Crock Pot Slow Cooker Cookbook

Low Sodium and Heart-Healthy Recipes for Your Slow Cooker.

Save Time and Money with this Easy to Follow Cookbook.

Tasty Dishes like a Restaurant without Stress.

Alexangel Kitchen

To Thank You for Purchasing the Book, for a limited time, you can get a Special FREE BOOK from Alexangel Kitchen

Free Book Here

Just go to https://alexangelkitchen.com/ **to download your FREE BOOK**

Table of Contents_Toc61170009

Introduction **9**

Meat...**13**

Island Lamb Stew...14

Steak Pizzaiola...17

Sweet and Spicy Meatballs.................................19

Beef Ragu 20

Corned Beef and Cabbage 22

Ancho-Beef Stew 24

Cider Braised Beef Pot Roast 26

Cajun Pot Roast.. 28

Sloppy Joes..31

Moroccan Beef Lettuce Wraps.......................... 33

Steak Fajitas 35

Beef and Eggplant 37

Barbecue Pulled Beef 39

Chili with Beef.. 42

Beef and Sweet Potato Massaman.................... 44

Stuffed Tomatoes with Meat and Cheese 46

Beef Taco Filling 48

Garlic Herb Pork 49

Garlic Thyme Lamb Chops 51

Pork Tenderloin 53

Smoky Pork with Cabbage 55

Roasted Pork Shoulder 57

Chili Lime Beef 58

Beef in Sauce 60

Beef with Greens 62

Beef and Scallions Bowl 63

Beef and Artichokes Bowls 65

Mustard Beef 66

Beef Masala 67

Beef Sauté with Endives 69

Sweet Beef 70

Thyme Beef 71

Hot Beef 72

Beef Chops with Sprouts 73

Beef Ragout with Beans 76

Coconut Beef 77

Pork Roast with Cheese 78

Pork Butt Carnitas..80

Pork Filled Avocado 83

Pork Tomatillo Salsa 85

Lamb and Spinach 86

Lamb and Leeks 88

Pumpkin Beef Chili 91

Chipotle Barbacoa Recipe... 93

Ground Pork and Veggies 96

Herbed Lamb Loin Chops..98

Savory Lamb Chili... 99

Wine Dipped Pork Ribs 102

Ground Beef and Broccoli... 104

Lamb Curry 105

Beef Stuffed Mushrooms 107

Southwest Jalapeno Beef.. 109

Lemon Beef 111

Caraway Ribs 113

Dinner Lamb Shanks 116

Mint Lamb Roast 118

Introduction

The crockpot has long been a favorite kitchen implement for the 'set-it-and-forget-it' meal. It's a wonderful invention by whoever thought it up, and it has saved many a few dollars on electricity by not needing to keep the stove and oven on for extended hours and all day. So, what really is a crockpot?

A crockpot is also called a slow cooker or a casserole crockpot. These nicknames refer to the same kitchen appliance, and it is one of the most used reheating methods today. It is basically a cooker with a glazed ceramic bowl that has a tight sealing lid. It is because of the liquid that will go in with the food. The crockpot is then plugged into an electrical socket in the kitchen for it to work.

The crockpot slow cooking method involves basically depositing the ingredients you desire to cook into the crockpot bowl (usually by stirring it with a wooden spoon or a ladle), adding the liquid of choice, cooking it for a few hours until it's done. These used to be the standard cooking methods in kitchens, and they have stayed the same with the invention of the crockpot. Nowadays, most crockpots have interiors thermostatically controlled to ensure that it's set at the right temperature during the cooking process to not over-cook your meals.

The best in crockpot slow cooking is finding that low and slow recipe. Recipes that are low in time length are usually very low in steps, and not much work is involved. It usually leads to the much sought after 'set it and forget it' kind of meal. Imagine not having to watch your meals cook slowly as you work on other tasks; you can avoid the temptation of peeking or checking on it too often and not having to worry about burning or crusting on the sides of your crockpot. When cooking at low heat, you don't have to worry about your meal exploding all over the kitchen or all the grease falling out and sticking to the bottom of your crock.

The best use of crockpot slow cooking is the convenience of the food, especially during holidays and parties. You can set the crockpot down on the table, and everyone can serve themselves. It is an excellent and great way to spend time with your guests and treat them well. There is nothing cheesier than eating the same dish fondue style. You get to enjoy slow cooking hotdogs for hours and hours without little ones surreptitiously taking off the top and poaching them in the pool of oil sitting beside the dish.

A crockpot is a very good way to use leftovers for a delicious meal. If you cook a large meal regularly and you have leftovers, put them in a crockpot with a liquid and let it cook. It will double the amount of food leftover or fed to the cat at the end of the week.

Crockpot cooking generally saves time, but it is also a low-budget way to cook. Slow cooking food can save you money because they are usually very low and easy to make. In fact, it is even possible to cook a meal with the last few pennies in your wallet. If you're on a tight budget and you don't have much to spend on your meals, the crockpot is the way to go. Crockpots even make for a great gift since it's made in many shapes and sizes, from the really small, 1-quart crockpot to the huge 8 quarts or more. Any shape or size would be a welcome gift for anyone because everyone eats. Any occasion could be a good time to give someone a crockpot, and the more occasions you can name, the more crockpots you could make as gifts. Crockpots are a good thing for singles who do not have many friends, and getting together can be difficult. You can go on cooking and not having to worry about cooking for anyone. You also don't have to go through the motions of doing a dinner party or charity work every week. You could just throw some ingredients together in your crockpot, turn it on and leave. That way, you're free to do whatever you like while your crockpot cooks your meal.

To whom is this cookbook? This cookbook is for people who want to spend less time in the kitchen and less money on food. This cookbook is also for people who wish to cook their meals in a healthy manner or for people with little time or money, and lastly, this is for people who enjoy sharing meals with friends and family. Treat your guests to a good meal every day. Slow cooking, live long!

MEAT

Island Lamb Stew

Preparation time: 15 minutes
Cooking time: 8 hours
Servings: 4
Ingredients:

- 1 tablespoon butter

- 1 cup onion, sliced

- 1 pound lamb, diced

- 1 cup celery, sliced

- ¾ cup green pepper, chopped

- 1 tablespoon curry powder

- 1 can tomatoes

- salt and pepper to taste

Directions:

1. Set the crockpot to high heat and add butter. Sauté the onions for a minute then add the lamb. Sear the lamb for 3 minutes.

2. Pour the remaining ingredients. Close the lid and set the heat to low. Cook for 8 hours.

Nutrition:

Calories: 352

Carbohydrates: 7.83g

Protein: 29.32g

Fat: 22.4 g

Steak Pizzaiola

Preparation time: 15 minutes

Cooking time: 8 hours & 20 minutes

Servings: 4

Ingredients:

- 12 oz flank steak

- 1 sweet bell pepper, de-seeded and sliced

- 2 tablespoons Italian seasoning

- 12 oz pasta sauce, sugar-free

- 4 oz shredded mozzarella cheese

Directions:

1. Grease a 4-quart crock pot with a non-stick cooking spray. Season the beef with salt, ground black pepper, and Italian seasoning, place in the crock pot, then pour in the pasta sauce.

2. Top with peppers and cover the crock pot with its lid. Set the cooking timer for 6 to 8 hours, and allow to cook at a low heat setting.

3. Remove the beef, and keep warm. Add the mozzarella to the crock pot, allowing to melt, but cooking for a further 20 minutes. To serve, slice the beef, and serve alongside the tomato mixture.

Nutrition:

Calories: 211

Carbohydrates: 4 g

Fats: 9.4 g

Protein: 26.3 g

Sweet and Spicy Meatballs

Preparation time: 15 minutes

Cooking time: 8 hours

Servings: 4

Ingredients:

- 12 oz meatballs

- 14 oz chili sauce, sugar-free

- 12 oz raspberry jam, sugar-free

Directions:

1. Grease a 4-quart crock pot with a non-stick cooking spray, and place the meatballs inside. Stir the chili sauce and the jam together in a bowl, then add to the crock pot.

2. Cover the crock pot with its lid, and set the cooking timer for 8 hours, allowing to cook at a low heat setting. Serve with cauliflower rice.

Nutrition:

Calories: 92

Carbohydrates: 4.5 g

Carbs: 3.9 g

Fats: 5.1 g

Protein: 7 g

Beef Ragu

Preparation time: 15 minutes

Cooking time: 8 hours & 5 minutes

Servings: 8

Ingredients:

- 12 oz beef short ribs, trimmed and cut into chunks

- 1 cup white onion, peeled and sliced

- 4 cups chopped tomatoes

- 3 tablespoons tomato paste, sugar-free

- 1 teaspoon dried basil and dried oregano

Directions:

1. Season the beef with salt and ground black pepper. Place a large skillet over a medium heat, add a tablespoon of olive oil, then add the beef pieces.

2. Allow to cook for 4 to 5 minutes, turning until all sides are seared. Grease a 4-quart crock pot with a non-stick cooking spray and add the remaining ingredients, mixing well.

3. Add the seared beef pieces, and place the lid on the crock pot. Allow to cook for 6 to 8 hours at a low heat setting.

4. Shred the beef with forks, and return it to the cooking liquid. Allow it to sit for 15 minutes. Garnish with grated cheese, and serve with zucchini noodles.

Nutrition:

Calories: 513.4

Carbohydrates: 12.4 g

Fats: 29.7 g

Protein: 45.8 g

Corned Beef and Cabbage

Preparation time: 15 minutes

Cooking time: 6 hours

Servings: 12

Ingredients:

- 6 lb. corned beef brisket

- 4 medium-sized carrots, peeled and cut into bite-size pieces

- 8 cups shredded cabbage

- 1 corned beef spiced packet

- 6 cups water

Directions:

1. Rub the meat with the corned beef spice packet. Grease a 4-quart crock pot with a non-stick cooking spray and add the carrots and the cabbage.

2. Pour in water, then top with the seasoned beef. Cover the crock pot with its lid, and set the cooking timer for 6 hours allowing to cook at a low heat. Serve the meat immediately, with the vegetables alongside.

Nutrition:

Calories: 334

Carbohydrates: 8.1 g

Fats: 22.8 g

Protein: 24.7 g

Ancho-Beef Stew

Preparation time: 15 minutes

Cooking time: 10 hours & 7 minutes

Servings: 4

Ingredients:

- 8 oz boneless beef chuck pot roast, trimmed

- 16 oz low-carb vegetables

- 1 tablespoon ground ancho-chili pepper

- 12 oz tomato salsa, sugar-free

- 1 1/2 cups of beef broth

Directions:

1. Cut meat into bite-size pieces and season on all sides with the ancho-chili pepper. Place a large non-stick skillet pan over medium-high heat, add 1 tablespoon olive oil, then the seasoned beef.

2. Allow to cook for 5 to 7 minutes, or until browned on all sides. Depending on the size of your pan, you can cook the beef chunks in batches.

3. Grease a 4-quart crock pot with a non-stick cooking spray and add the vegetables. Top with the browned meat and season with salt and ground black pepper.

4. Stir in the tomato salsa and the beef broth, then cover the crock pot with its lid. Set the cooking timer for 8 to 10 hours, allowing the meat to cook at a low heat setting or until meat is cooked through. Serve the meat warm, with the vegetables alongside.

Nutrition:

Calories: 288

Carbohydrates: 8 g

Fats: 20 g

Protein: 20 g

Cider Braised Beef Pot Roast

Preparation time: 15 minutes

Cooking time: 8 hours & 10 minutes

Servings: 4

Ingredients:

- 8 oz boneless chuck pot roast, trimmed

- 1/2 cup chopped white onion

- 1 teaspoon garlic powder

- 1/4 cup apple cider vinegar

- 1/4 teaspoon xanthan gum

Directions:

1. Season the chuck roast with the garlic powder, salt, and ground black pepper. Place a large non-stick skillet pan over medium-high heat, add a tablespoon of olive oil, then add the meat.

2. Allow to cook for 7 to 10 minutes, turning until it has browned on all sides. Grease a 4-quart crock pot with a non-stick cooking spray and add the browned meat.

3. Top with the onion and pour in the vinegar and 1 1/2 cups of water. Cover the crock pot with its lid, and set the cooking timer for 8 hours, allowing the meat to cook at a low heat setting.

4. Place the meat on a plate, then shred using forks, and keep warm. Transfer the remaining mixture to a saucepan, add the xanthan gum, and bring to boil, allowing to cook until sauce reduces to the desired thickness. Serve the meat with the sauce alongside.

Nutrition:

Calories: 393

Carbohydrates: 4 g

Fats: 28 g

Protein: 30 g

Cajun Pot Roast

Preparation time: 15 minutes

Cooking time: 8 hours

Servings: 8

Ingredients:

- 18 oz boneless beef chuck roast, trimmed

- 1 white onion, peeled and chopped

- 14 oz diced tomatoes with garlic,

- 1 tablespoon Cajun seasoning,

- 1 teaspoon Tabasco sauce

Directions:

1. Season the beef on all sides with the Cajun seasoning mix. Grease a 4-quart crock pot with a non-stick cooking spray, add the seasoned beef, and top with the onion.

2. In a bowl, stir together the tomato with garlic, the Tabasco sauce and a pinch of salt and ground black pepper. Pour the tomato mixture over the vegetables and beef, then cover the crock pot with its lid.

3. Set the cooking timer for 6 to 8 hours, and allow to cook at a low heat setting. To serve, transfer the beef to a

serving platter, then top with onion and tomato mixture.

Nutrition:

Calories: 314 Kcal

Carbohydrates: 10.4 g

Fats: 15.1 g

Protein: 38 g

Sloppy Joes

Preparation time: 15 minutes

Cooking time: 8 hours & 10 minutes

Servings: 6

Ingredients:

- 1 lb. ground beef

- 2 tablespoons Worcestershire sauce

- 1 tablespoon Dijon mustard

- 1 cup Picante Sauce, sugar-free

- 3/4 cup hot barbecue sauce, sugar-free

Directions:

1. Place a large non-stick skillet pan over medium-high heat, and add the beef. Cook for 8 to 10 minutes, stirring regularly, until the meat is no longer pink.

2. Drain the fat from the mixture, and transfer to a 4-quart crock pot. Stir in the remaining ingredients, and season with salt and black pepper.

3. Seal the crock pot with its lid, then set the cooking timer for 6 to 8 hours, allow the mixture to cook at a low heat setting.

4. To serve, place a generous helping of the mixture on a roasted Portobello mushroom caps, and top with a second Portobello mushroom cap.

Nutrition:

Calories: 162.5

Carbohydrates: 2.5 g

Fats: 4.5 g

Protein: 24 g

Moroccan Beef Lettuce Wraps

Preparation time: 15 minutes

Cooking time: 10 hours

Servings: 4

Ingredients:

- 12 oz beef roast, trimmed and cut into bite-size pieces

- 1 cup sliced white onions

- 1 teaspoon sea salt

- 4 tablespoons garam masala,

- 10 large lettuce leaves, for wrapping

Directions:

1. Grease a 4-quart crock pot and add all the ingredients apart from the lettuce. Cover and seal crock pot with its lid. Set the cooking timer for 8 hours and allow to cook at a low heat setting.

2. Remove the beef, and shred it using forks. Place the meat back in the crock pot, and continue cooking for another 2 hours. Serve warm, wrapped in the lettuce leaves.

Nutrition:

Calories: 209

Carbohydrates: 0.7 g

Fats: 9.5 g

Protein: 30.4 g

Steak Fajitas

Preparation time: 15 minutes

Cooking time: 4 hours

Servings: 4

Ingredients:

- 16 oz flank steak

- 1 red and 1 green bell pepper, de-seeded and sliced

- 1 white onion, peeled and sliced

- 2 tablespoons fajita seasoning,

- 20 oz tomato salsa, sugar-free

Directions:

1. Grease a 4-quart crock pot with a non-stick cooking spray and then pour the salsa in. Place the peppers and onion on top, and sprinkle with the fajita seasoning.

2. Stir until mixed well, then cover and seal the crock pot with its lid. Set the cooking timer for 3 to 4 hours, and allow to cook at a high heat setting. Serve with shredded cheese and sour cream.

Nutrition:

Calories: 222

Carbohydrates: 5 g

Fats: 12 g

Protein: 23 g

Beef and Eggplant

Preparation time: 15 minutes

Cooking time: 4 hours & 30 minutes

Servings: 6

Ingredients:

- 2 lb. ground beef

- 3 cans of chopped tomatoes

- 2 medium-sized eggplants, de-stemmed

- 3 tablespoons Lebanese Spice Blend

- 2 cups shredded mozzarella cheese

Directions:

1. Cut the eggplant into large chunks and add to a 4-quart crock pot, greased with non-stick cooking spray.

2. Stir together the ground beef and the spice blend, and season with salt and ground black pepper. Place this over the eggplant.

3. Pour over the chopped tomato, then place the lid on the crock pot. Set the cooking timer for 4 hours and allow to cook at a low heat setting.

4. Add the shredded mozzarella, and allow to cook for a further 30 minutes, until the cheese is melted. Garnish with parsley to serve.

Nutrition:

Calories: 209

Carbohydrates: 8.1 g

Fats: 12.8 g

Protein: 15.9 g

Barbecue Pulled Beef

Preparation time: 15 minutes

Cooking time: 4 hours

Servings: 4

Ingredients:

- 12 oz beef pot roast, trimmed and cut into bite sized pieces
- 1 teaspoon minced garlic
- 1 teaspoon onion powder
- 1/4 cup apple cider vinegar
- 3/4 cup tomato ketchup, sugar-free

Directions:

1. Grease a 4-quart crock pot with a non-stick cooking spray. Mix together all of the ingredients, apart from the beef, and place the mixture in the crock pot.

2. Add the beef pieces, and season with a pinch of salt and ground black pepper. Cover and seal the crock pot with its lid, setting the cooking timer for 4 hours, and allowing to cook at a high heat setting.

3. Shred the meat with forks, and serve between roasted Portobello mushroom caps.

Nutrition:

Calories: 380

Carbohydrates: 6 g

Fats: 15 g

Protein: 49 g

Chili with Beef

Preparation time: 15 minutes

Cooking time: 8 hours & 7 minutes

Servings: 6

Ingredients:

- 1 lb. ground beef

- 2 cans diced tomatoes with green chilies

- 2 white onions, diced

- 4 garlic cloves, minced

- 1 1/2 tablespoon Mexican seasoning

- 6 oz tomato paste

Directions:

1. Place a large skillet pan over medium-high heat, add the beef, half of both the garlic and the onion, and a pinch of salt and ground black pepper.

2. Cook for 5 to 7 minutes, stirring regularly, until the meat is nicely golden brown. Drain off the fat, and add to the crock pot.

3. Stir in remaining ingredients, and place the lid on the crock pot. Set the cooking timer for 6 to 8 hours, and allow to cook at a low heat setting. To serve, allow

people to help themselves to cilantro, grated cheese and sour cream.

Nutrition:

Calories: 306

Carbohydrates: 13 g

Fats: 18 g

Protein: 23 g

Beef and Sweet Potato Massaman

Preparation time: 15 minutes

Cooking time: 8 hours

Servings: 6

Ingredients:

- 3 lb. beef roast, cut into large pieces, and coated with coconut flour

- 12 oz sweet potato, peeled and cut into bite-size pieces

- 2 red onions, peeled and sliced

- 1/2 cup Massaman curry powder

- 1 can full-fat coconut cream

Directions:

1. Grease a 4-quarts crock pot with a non-stick cooking spray, and place all of the ingredients inside, stirring until mixed. Add 2 cups of water or chicken broth, mixing this through evenly.

2. Seal the crock pot with its lid, and set the cooking timer for 8 hours, allowing the food to cook at a low heat setting. Remove the meat, and shred with forks, then transfer to the serving dish.

3. Top with the onions and sweet potatoes, drizzle with the sauce, and garnish with coriander. Serve with cooked cauliflower rice.

Nutrition:

Calories: 256

Carbohydrates: 2 g

Fats: 14.1 g

Protein: 29.1 g

Stuffed Tomatoes with Meat and Cheese

Preparation time: 15 minutes

Cooking time: 4 hours

Servings: 6

Ingredients:

- 12 oz sausage meat

- 6 plum tomatoes

- 2 cans tomatoes with basil

- 3 tablespoons Italian seasoning

- 1 1/4 cup grated Monterey Jack cheese

Directions:

1. Cut a thin slice from the top end of each tomato, then use a spoon to remove the seeds.

2. Mix together the sausage meat, the Italian seasoning, and a pinch of salt and ground black pepper, then fill each tomato with the meat mixture. Sprinkle each one with cheese.

3. Grease a 4-quarts crock pot with a non-stick cooking spray and pour in the tomatoes with basil. Arrange the stuffed tomatoes on top, then place the lid on the crock pot.

4. Set the cooking timer for 4 hours, allowing the food to cook on a low heat setting. Serve warm.

Nutrition:

Calories: 286

Carbohydrates: 7.9 g

Fats: 23.3 g

Protein: 18.7 g

Beef Taco Filling

Preparation time: 10 minutes

Cooking time: 6 hours

Servings: 12

Ingredients

- 1 lb. ground beef

- 1 can tomato with green chilies

- 1 envelope taco seasoning

Directions:

1. Add all Ingredients: to the crockpot and stir well. Cover crockpot with lid and cook on low for 6 hours. Serve and enjoy.

Nutrition:

Calories 75

Fat 2.4 g

Carbohydrates 0.9 g

Protein 11.7 g

Garlic Herb Pork

Preparation time: 10 minutes

Cooking time: 8 hours

Servings: 10

Ingredients

- 1 lbs. pork shoulder roast, boneless and cut into 4 pieces

- ½ tbsp. cumin

- ½ tbsp. fresh oregano

- 2/3 cup grapefruit juice

- garlic cloves

- Pepper and salt

Directions:

1. Add pork roast into the crockpot. Season with pepper and salt. Add garlic, cumin, oregano, and grapefruit juice into the blender and blend until smooth.

2. Pour blended mixture over pork and stir well. Cover crockpot with lid and cook on low for 8 hours. Remove pork from the crockpot and shred using a fork.

3. Return shredded pork into the crockpot and stir well. Serve warm and enjoy.

Nutrition:

Calories 359

Fat 27.8 g

Carbohydrates 2.1 g

Protein 23.2 g

Garlic Thyme Lamb Chops

Preparation time: 10 minutes

Cooking time: 6 hours

Servings: 8

Ingredients

- 1 pound lamb chops

- 1 tsp dried oregano

- 2 garlic cloves, minced

- ½ tsp dried thyme

- 1 medium onion, sliced

- Pepper and salt

Directions:

1. Add sliced onion into the crockpot. Combine together thyme, oregano, pepper, and salt. Rub over lamb chops. Place lamb chops in the crockpot and top with garlic.

2. Pour ¼ cup water around the lamb chops. Cover crockpot with lid and cook on low for 6 hours. Serve and enjoy.

Nutrition:

Calories 40

Fat 1.9 g

Carbohydrates 2.3 g

Protein 3.4 g

Pork Tenderloin

Preparation time: 10 minutes

Cooking time: 4 hours

Servings: 6

Ingredients

- 1 ½ lbs. pork tenderloin, trimmed and cut in half lengthwise

- garlic cloves, chopped

- 1 oz envelope dry onion soup mix

- ¾ cup red wine

- 1 cup water

- Pepper and salt

Directions:

1. Place pork tenderloin into the crockpot. Pour red wine and water over pork. Sprinkle dry onion soup mix on top of pork tenderloin.

2. Top with chopped garlic and season with pepper and salt. Cover crockpot with lid and cook on low for 4 hours. Stir well and serve.

Nutrition:

Calories 196

Fat 4 g

Carbohydrates 3.1 g

Protein 29.9 g

Smoky Pork with Cabbage

Preparation time: 10 minutes

Cooking time: 8 hours

Servings: 6

Ingredients

- 1 lbs. pastured pork roast

- 1/3 cup liquid smoke

- 1/2 cabbage head, chopped

- 1 cup water

- 1 tbsp. kosher salt

Directions:

1. Rub pork with kosher salt and place into the crockpot. Pour liquid smoke over the pork. Add water. Cover crockpot with lid and cook on low for 7 hours.

2. Remove pork from the crockpot and add cabbage to the bottom of the crockpot. Now place pork on top of the cabbage.

3. Cover again and cook for 1 hour more. Shred pork with a fork and serves.

Nutrition:

Calories 484

Fat 21.5 g

Carbohydrates 3.5 g

Protein 65.4 g

Roasted Pork Shoulder

Preparation time: 10 minutes

Cooking time: 9 hours

Servings: 8

Ingredients

- 1 lbs. pork shoulder

- 1 tsp garlic powder

- 1/2 cup water

- 1/2 tsp black pepper

- 1/2 tsp sea salt

Directions:

1. Season pork with garlic powder, pepper, and salt and place in a crockpot. Add water. Cover crockpot with lid and cook on high for 1 hour, then turn heat to low and cook for 8 hours.

2. Remove meat from the crockpot and shred using a fork. Serve and enjoy.

Nutrition:

Calories 664

Fat 48.5 g

Carbohydrates 0.3 g

Protein 52.9 g

Chili Lime Beef

Preparation time: 10 minutes

Cooking time: 6 hours

Servings: 4

Ingredients

- 1 lb. beef chuck roast

- 1 tsp chili powder

- 2 cups lemon-lime soda

- 1 fresh lime juice

- 1 garlic clove, crushed

- 1/2 tsp salt

Directions:

1. Place beef chuck roast into the crockpot. Season roast with garlic, chili powder, and salt. Pour lemon-lime soda over the roast.

2. Cover crockpot with lid and cook on low for 6 hours. Shred the meat using a fork. Add lime juice over shredded roast and serve.

Nutrition:

Calories 355

Fat 16.8 g

Carbohydrates 14 g

Protein 35.5 g

Beef in Sauce

Preparation time: 10 minutes

Cooking time: 9 hours

Servings: 4

Ingredients

- 1-pound beef stew meat, chopped

- 1 teaspoon gram masala

- 1 cup of water

- 1 tablespoon flour

- 1 teaspoon garlic powder

- 1 onion, diced

Directions

1. Whisk flour with water until smooth and pour the liquid into the crockpot. Add gram masala and beef stew meat.

2. After this, add onion and garlic powder. Close the lid and cook the meat on low for 9 hours. Serve the cooked beef with thick gravy from the crockpot.

Nutrition:

Calories 231

Protein 35g

Carbohydrates 4.6g

Fat 7.1g

Beef with Greens

Preparation time: 15 minutes

Cooking time: 8 hours

Servings: 3

Ingredients:

- 1 cup fresh spinach, chopped

- 1 pound beef stew meat, cubed

- 1 cup Swiss chard, chopped

- 2 cups of water

- 1 teaspoon olive oil

- 1 teaspoon dried rosemary

Directions:

1. Heat olive oil in the skillet. Add beef and roast it for 1 minute per side. Then transfer the meat to the crockpot.

2. Add Swiss chard, spinach, water, and rosemary. Close the lid and cook the meal on Low for 8 hours.

Nutrition:

Calories 177

Protein 26.3g

Carbohydrates 1.1g

Fat 7g

Beef and Scallions Bowl

Preparation time: 10 minutes

Cooking time: 5 hours

Servings: 4

Ingredients

- 1 teaspoon chili powder

- 2 oz. scallions, chopped

- 1-pound beef stew meat, cubed

- 1 cup corn kernels, frozen

- 1 cup of water

- 2 tablespoons tomato paste

- 1 teaspoon minced garlic

Directions

1. Mix water with tomato paste and pour the liquid into the crockpot. Add chili powder, beef, corn kernels, and minced garlic.

2. Close the lid and cook the meal on high for 5 hours. When the meal is cooked, transfer the mixture to the bowls and top with scallions.

Nutrition:

Calories 258

Protein 36.4g

Carbohydrates 0.4g

Fat 7.7g

Beef and Artichokes Bowls

Preparation time: 10 minutes

Cooking time: 7 hours

Servings: 2

Ingredients

- 1 pound beef sirloin, chopped

- ½ teaspoon cayenne pepper

- ½ teaspoon white pepper

- artichoke hearts, chopped

- 1 cup of water

- 1 teaspoon salt

Directions

1. Mix meat with white pepper and cayenne pepper. Transfer it to the crockpot bowl. Add salt, artichoke hearts, and water. Close the lid and cook the meal on Low for 7 hours.

Nutrition:

Calories 313

Protein 36.5g

Carbohydrates 4.6g

Fat 5.9g

Mustard Beef

Preparation time: 10 minutes

Cooking time: 8 hours

Servings: 4

Ingredients:

- 1-pound beef sirloin, chopped

- 1 tablespoon capers, drained

- 1 cup of water

- 2 tablespoons mustard

- 1 tablespoon coconut oil

Directions:

1. Mix meat with mustard and leave for 10 minutes to marinate. Then melt the coconut oil in the skillet. Add meat and roast it for 1 minute per side on high heat.

2. After this, transfer the meat to the crockpot. Add water and capers. Cook the meal on Low for 8 hours.

Nutrition:

Calories 267

Protein 35.9g

Carbohydrates 2.1g

Fat 12.1g

Beef Masala

Preparation time: 15 minutes

Cooking time: 9 hours

Servings: 6

Ingredients

- 1-pound beef sirloin, sliced

- 1 teaspoon gram masala

- 2 tablespoons lemon juice

- 1 teaspoon ground paprika

- ½ cup of coconut milk

- 1 teaspoon dried mint

Directions

1. In the bowl, mix coconut milk with dried mint, ground paprika, lemon juice, and gram masala. Then add beef sirloin and mix the mixture.

2. Leave it for at least 10 minutes to marinate. Then transfer the mixture to the crockpot. Cook it on Low for 9 hours.

Nutrition:

Calories 283

Protein 35.3g

Carbohydrates 2.2g

Fat 14.4g

Beef Sauté with Endives

Preparation time: 10 minutes

Cooking time: 8 hours

Servings: 4

Ingredients:

- 1-pound beef sirloin, chopped

- 1 oz. endives, roughly chopped

- 1 teaspoon peppercorns

- 1 carrot, diced

- 1 onion, sliced

- 1 cup of water

- ½ cup tomato juice

Directions:

1. Mix beef with onion, carrot, and peppercorns. Place the mixture in the crockpot. Add water and tomato juice.

2. Then close the lid and cook it on High for 5 hours. After this, add endives and cook the meal for 3 hours on Low.

Nutrition:

Calories 238

Protein 35.4g

Carbohydrates 6.4g

Fat 7.2g

Sweet Beef

Preparation time: 10 minutes

Cooking time: 5 hours

Servings: 4

Ingredients:

- 1-pound beef roast, sliced

- 1 tablespoon maple syrup

- 2 tablespoons lemon juice

- 1 teaspoon dried oregano

- 1 cup of water

Directions:

1. Mix water with maple syrup, lemon juice, and dried oregano. Then pour the liquid into the crockpot. Add beef roast and close the lid. Cook the meal on High for 5 hours.

Nutrition:

Calories 227

Protein 34.5g

Carbohydrates 3.8g

Fat 7.2g

Thyme Beef

Preparation time: 15 minutes

Cooking time: 5 hours

Servings: 2

Ingredients:

- 1 pound beef sirloin, chopped

- 1 tablespoon dried thyme

- 1 tablespoon olive oil

- ½ cup of water

- 1 teaspoon salt

Directions:

1. Preheat the skillet well. Then mix beef with dried thyme and olive oil. Put the meat in the hot skillet and roast for 2 minutes per side on high heat.

2. Then transfer the meat to the crockpot. Add salt and water. Cook the meal on High for 5 hours.

Nutrition:

Calories 274

Protein 34.5g

Carbohydrates 0.9g

Fat 14.2g

Hot Beef

Preparation time: 15 minutes

Cooking time: 8 hours

Servings: 4

Ingredients:

- 1-pound beef sirloin, chopped

- 2 tablespoons hot sauce

- 1 tablespoon olive oil

- ½ cup of water

Directions:

1. In the shallow bowl, mix hot sauce with olive oil. Then mix beef sirloin with hot sauce mixture and leave for 10 minutes to marinate.

2. Put the marinated beef in the crockpot. Add water and close the lid. Cook the meal on Low for 8 hours.

Nutrition:

Calories 241

Protein 34.4g

Carbohydrates 0.1g

Fat 10.6g

Beef Chops with Sprouts

Preparation time: 10 minutes

Cooking time: 7 hours

Servings: 5

Ingredients:

- 1-pound beef loin

- ½ cup bean sprouts

- 1 cup of water

- 1 tablespoon tomato paste

- 1 teaspoon chili powder

- 1 teaspoon salt

Directions:

1. Cut the beef loin into 5 beef chops and sprinkle the beef chops with chili powder and salt. Then place them in the crockpot.

2. Add water and tomato paste. Cook the meat on low for 7 hours. Then transfer the cooked beef chops onto the plates, sprinkle with tomato gravy from the crockpot, and top with bean sprouts.

Nutrition:

Calories 175

Protein 5.2g

Carbohydrates 1.6g

Fat 7.8g

Beef Ragout with Beans

Preparation time: 10 minutes

Cooking time: 5 hours

Servings: 5

Ingredients:

- 1 tablespoon tomato paste

- 1 cup mug beans, canned

- 1 carrot, grated

- 1-pound beef stew meat, chopped

- 1 teaspoon ground black pepper

- 2 cups of water

Directions:

1. Pour water into the crockpot. Add meat, ground black pepper, and carrot. Cook the mixture on High for 4 hours. Then add tomato paste and mug beans. Stir the meal and cook it on high for 1 hour more.

Nutrition:

Calories 321

Protein 37.7g

Carbohydrates 28g

Fat 6.2g

7.3g fiber,

Coconut Beef

Preparation time: 10 minutes

Cooking time: 8 hours

Servings: 5

Ingredients:

- 1 cup baby spinach, chopped

- 1 cup of coconut milk

- 1-pound beef tenderloin, chopped

- 1 teaspoon avocado oil

- 1 teaspoon dried rosemary

- 1 teaspoon garlic powder

Directions:

1. Roast meat in the avocado oil for 1 minute per side on high heat. Then transfer the meat in the crockpot.

2. Add garlic powder, dried rosemary, coconut milk, and baby spinach. Close the lid and cook the meal on Low for 8 hours.

Nutrition:

Calories 303

Protein 27.6g

Carbohydrates 3.5g

Fat 19.9g

Pork Roast with Cheese

Preparation time: 15 minutes

Cooking Time: 6 Hours 5 Minutes

Servings: 2

Ingredients:

- 1 1/2 cups of chicken stock

- 1 cup of diced onion

- 1/2 cup of diced mushrooms

- 3 4 celery stalks, diced

- 1/4 cup of parsley, dried

- 1/2 stick butter

- 2 teaspoons of salt

- 1 teaspoon of garlic powder

- 1 teaspoon of black pepper

For the Gravy:

- 1 cup of heavy cream

- 4 oz. cream cheese, cubed

- 1/2 stick butter

- 1/2 1 teaspoon of Glucomannan powder

- 1 1/2 2 cups of cooking liquid from the roast

Directions:

1. Start by putting all the fixings except those for the gravy into your Crockpot. Cover its lid and cook for 6 hours on high setting. Once done, remove its lid and mix well.

2. Mix all the gravy Ingredients: in a saucepan and stir cook for 5 minutes. Pour this gravy over the slow-cooked pork. Garnish as desired. Serve warm.

Nutrition:

Calories 359

Fat 34 g

Carbs 8.5 g

Protein 27.5 g

Pork Butt Carnitas

Preparation time: 15 minutes

Cooking Time: 8 Hours

Servings: 8

Ingredients:

- ½ tablespoon of black pepper

- 1 tablespoon of chili powder

- 1 tablespoon of bacon grease

- 1 small onion

- 1 tablespoon of cumin

- 1 tablespoon of thyme, dried

- 4 lb. pork butt

- 2 tablespoons of garlic, minced

- ½ cup of water

Directions:

1. Start by putting all the fixings into your Crockpot. Cover its lid and cook for 8 hours on High setting. Once done, remove its lid and mix well. Garnish as desired. Serve warm.

Nutrition:

Calories 329

Fat 34 g

Carbs 6.5 g

Protein 27.5 g

Pork Filled Avocado

Preparation time: 15 minutes

Cooking Time: 4 Hours

Servings: 6

Ingredients:

- ½ tablespoon of cumin, ground

- 1 teaspoon of salt

- ½ tablespoon of chili powder

- ½ tablespoon of garlic powder

- ½ tablespoon of butter

- 6 avocados, cut in half, pits removed and scooped

Directions:

1. Start by putting all the fixings into your Crockpot except the avocados. Cover its lid and cook for 4 hours on High setting.

2. Once done, remove its lid and mix well. Shred the slow-cooked pork and return to the crockpot. Mix well and divide this mixture into the avocados. Garnish as desired. Serve warm.

Nutrition:

Calories 397

Fat 17.1 g

Carbs 1.9 g

Protein 41.2 g

Pork Tomatillo Salsa

Preparation time: 15 minutes

Cooking Time: 10 Hours

Servings: 8

Ingredients:

- Salt and black pepper to taste

- 4 teaspoon of Garlic powder

- 2 tablespoon of Olive oil

- 36 oz. Green chili tomatillo salsa

Directions:

1. Start by putting all the fixings into your Crockpot. Cover its lid and cook for 10 hours on medium setting. Once done, remove its lid and mix well. Garnish as desired. Serve warm.

Nutrition:

Calories 274

Fat 13 g

Carbs 8.5 g

Protein 25.1 g

Lamb and Spinach

Preparation time: 15 minutes

Cooking Time: 8 Hours

Servings: 4

Ingredients:

- 1 teaspoon cumin, ground

- 1 tablespoon olive oil

- ¼ teaspoon chili powder

- ½ teaspoon black pepper

- ½ teaspoon salt

- 1-pound lamb chops

- ½ cup fresh spinach

- ¼ cup of water

Directions:

1. In the crockpot, mix the lamb with cumin, oil and the other ingredients except the spinach. Close the lid. Cook the rack of lamb for 7 hours on Low. Add the spinach, cook on Low for 1 hour, divide into bowls and serve.

Nutrition:

Calories 328

Fat 14.9g

Carbs 4.2g

Protein 23.3g

Lamb and Leeks

Preparation time: 15 minutes
Cooking Time: 6 Hours
Servings: 4
Ingredients:

- 3 oz leeks, roughly chopped

- 1-pound lamb chops

- 1 teaspoon dried basil

- 1 teaspoon Italian seasoning

- ½ teaspoon salt

- ½ teaspoon black pepper

- 1 teaspoon ground paprika

- 1 garlic clove, diced

- 2 spring onions, chopped

- ½ teaspoon chili pepper

- ¼ cup heavy cream

- 1 teaspoon olive oil

Directions:

1. In the crockpot, mix the lamb with leeks, basil, seasoning and the other ingredients. Close the lid. Cook the pot roast for 6 hours on High.

Nutrition:

Calories 296

Fat 14.3g

Carbs 6.6g

Protein 17.8g

Pumpkin Beef Chili

Preparation time: 15 minutes

Cooking Time: 3 Hours

Servings: 6

Ingredients:

- 1 green bell pepper, diced

- 1 ½ lb. Beef, ground

- 6 garlic cloves, minced

- 28 oz. canned tomatoes, diced

- 14 oz. pumpkin puree

- 1 cup of chicken stock

- 2 tablespoon of Chili powder

- 1 ½ teaspoon of Cumin, ground

- 1 teaspoon of Cinnamon powder

- Salt and black pepper- to taste

Directions:

1. Start by putting all the fixings into your Crockpot. Cover it and cook for 4 hours on Low settings. Once done, uncover the pot and mix well. Garnish as desired. Serve warm.

Nutrition:

Calories 238

Fat 13.8 g

Carbs 4.3 g

Protein 34.4g

Chipotle Barbacoa Recipe

Preparation time: 15 minutes

Cooking Time: 10 Hours

Servings: 6

Ingredients:

- 1/2 cup of beef broth

- 2 medium chipotle chilis in adobo

- 5 cloves garlic

- 2 tablespoons of apple cider vinegar

- 2 tablespoons of lime juice

- 1 tablespoon of oregano, dried

- 2 teaspoons of cumin

- 2 teaspoons of salt

- 1 teaspoon of black pepper

- 1/2 teaspoons of cloves, ground

- 2 whole bay leaf

Directions:

1. Start by putting all the fixings into your Crockpot. Cover it and cook for 10 hours on Low settings. Once done, uncover the pot and mix well. Shred the slow-cooked beef and return it to the pot. Serve warm.

Nutrition:

Calories 248

Protein 43.2 g

Fat 15.7 g

Ground Pork and Veggies

Preparation time: 15 minutes

Cooking Time: 8 Hours

Servings: 5

Ingredients:

- 2 cups ground pork

- 1 tablespoon minced garlic

- 1 green bell pepper, chopped

- 1 red bell pepper, chopped

- 1 zucchini, chopped

- 1 eggplant, chopped

- ½ cup cherry tomatoes, halved

- ½ cup keto tomato sauce

- 2 spring onions, chopped

- 1 teaspoon cayenne pepper

- ½ teaspoon salt

- ½ teaspoon ground coriander

- 1 tablespoon butter, softened

Directions:

1. In the crockpot, mix the pork with garlic, pepper and the other ingredients, toss, close the lid and cook for 8 hours on Low. Divide into bowls and serve.

Nutrition:

Calories 349

Fat 16.3g

Carbs 5.5g

Protein 13.8g

Herbed Lamb Loin Chops

Preparation time: 15 minutes

Cooking Time: 8 Hours

Servings: 1

Ingredients:

- 2 tablespoons of Butter melted

- 1 tablespoon of swerve

- ¼ cup of dill, diced

- 3 green onions, diced

- 1 tablespoon of Lemon peel, grated

- Salt and black pepper- to taste

- 1 lamb loin chop

Directions:

1. Start by putting all the fixings into your Crockpot. Cover its lid and cook for 8 hours on Low setting. Once done, remove its lid and mix well. Garnish as desired. Serve warm.

Nutrition:

Calories 298

Fat 14.4 g

Carbs 7.4 g

Protein 31.4 g

Savory Lamb Chili

Preparation time: 15 minutes

Cooking Time: 4 Hours

Servings: 6

Ingredients:

- 1 green bell pepper, diced

- 1 ½ lb. lamb ground

- 6 garlic cloves, minced

- 28 oz. canned tomatoes, diced

- 14 oz. pumpkin puree

- 1 cup of chicken stock

- 2 tablespoon of chili powder

- 1 ½ teaspoon of cumin, ground

- 1 teaspoon of cinnamon powder

- Salt and black pepper- to taste

Directions:

1. Start by putting all the fixings into your Crockpot. Cover it and cook for 5 hours on Low settings. Once done, uncover the pot and mix well. Garnish as desired. Serve warm.

Nutrition:

Calories 238

Fat 13.8 g

Carbs 4.3 g

Protein 34.4g

Wine Dipped Pork Ribs

Preparation time: 15 minutes

Cooking Time: 8.5 Hours

Servings: 4

Ingredients:

- ¾ teaspoon of erythritol

- ½ teaspoon of garlic powder

- ½ teaspoon of allspice

- ½ teaspoon of salt

- ¼ teaspoon of black pepper

- ½ teaspoon of onion powder

- ¼ teaspoon of coriander powder

- ¼ cup of tomato ketchup

- ¾ tablespoon of red wine vinegar

- ½ teaspoon of ground mustard

- ¼ teaspoon of liquid smoke

Directions:

1. Start by putting all the fixings into your Crockpot. Cover its lid and cook for 8 hours on Low setting. Once done, remove its lid and mix well.

2. Transfer the ribs to the serving plate. Cook the remaining sauce in the crockpot for 30 minutes on high heat. Pour this sauce over the ribs on the plate. Garnish as desired. Serve warm.

Nutrition:

Calories 244

Fat 17.4 g

Carbs 4.5 g

Protein 31.2 g

Ground Beef and Broccoli

Preparation time: 15 minutes

Cooking Time: 2 Hours

Servings: 4

Ingredients:

- 3 oz. butter

- ½ cup of beef stock

- 9 oz. broccoli, trimmed and diced

- Salt and black pepper-to taste

- ½ cup of mayonnaise or crème Fraiche

Directions:

1. Start by putting all the fixings into your Crockpot. Cover it and cook for 2 hours on Low settings. Once done, uncover the pot and mix well. Garnish as desired. Serve warm.

Nutrition:

Calories 272

Fat 18 g

Carbs 4 g

Protein 19.4 g

Lamb Curry

Preparation time: 15 minutes

Cooking Time: 8 Hours

Servings: 6 – 8

Ingredients:

- 2 ½ lb. boneless lamb (shoulder is a good cut to choose for this dish), cubed

- 2 onions, roughly chopped

- 5 garlic cloves, finely chopped

- 4 tbsp curry paste

- 1 lamb stock cube

- 2 ½ full-fat coconut milk

- 2 tomatoes, chopped

- Fresh coriander, roughly chopped

- Full-fat Greek yogurt, to serve

Directions:

1. Heat some oil in skillet or pan. Add the lamb to the hot pan and seal on all sides, about 3 minutes. Drizzle some olive oil into the crockpot.

2. Add the lamb, onions, garlic, curry paste, salt, and pepper to the pot. Stir to coat the lamb in curry paste.

Add the coconut milk, stock cube, chopped tomatoes, and 1 cup of water to the pot.

3. Place the lid onto the pot and set the temperature to LOW. Cook for 8 hours. Serve with a dollop of Greek yoghurt and fresh coriander.

Nutrition:

Calories: 144

Carbs: 7g

Fat: 6g

Protein: 14g

Beef Stuffed Mushrooms

Preparation time: 15 minutes

Cooking Time: 3 Hours

Servings: 4

Ingredients:

- 1 cup cremini mushroom caps

- ½ cup ground beef

- 1 tablespoon butter, soft

- 1 teaspoon coriander, ground

- 1 teaspoon sweet paprika

- 1 teaspoon dried dill

- 1 oz Parmesan, grated

- ¾ cup of water

Directions:

1. In a bowl, mix ground beef, butter, coriander, dill and paprika. Fill every mushroom cap with the meat mixture and arrange them in the crockpot. Add water.

2. Top every mushroom cap with Parmesan and close the lid. Cook the mushroom caps for 3 hours on High.

Nutrition:

Calories 260

Fat 5.8g

Carbs 8.6g

Protein 7.4g

Southwest Jalapeno Beef

Preparation time: 15 minutes

Cooking Time: 6 Hours

Servings: 4

Ingredients:

- 1 red onion, diced

- ½ green pepper, diced

- 2 oz. olive oil

- 10 oz. diced tomatoes

- 1 cup of carrots, diced

- 3 diced jalapeños

- 3 cup of cauliflower rice

- 3 cup of chicken stock

- 3 tablespoons of chili powder

- 1 tablespoon of salt

- 1 tablespoon of pepper

- 2 oz. diced cilantro

Directions:

1. Start by putting all the fixings into your Crockpot. Cover it and cook for 6 hours on Low settings. Once done, uncover the pot and mix well. Garnish as desired. Serve warm.

Nutrition:

Calories 391

Fat 21.8 g

Carbs 1.5 g

Protein 11.6 g

Lemon Beef

Preparation time: 15 minutes

Cooking Time: 5 Hours

Servings: 4

Ingredients:

- 1-pound beef sirloin, chopped

- 3 tablespoons lemon juice

- 1 teaspoon curry powder

- 1 teaspoon chili flakes

- 1 teaspoon lemon zest, grated

- ½ teaspoon salt

- 1 tablespoon keto tomato sauce

- 1 teaspoon butter

- ½ cup of water

- ½ teaspoon cayenne pepper

Directions:

1. In the crockpot, mix the beef with lemon juice and zest and the other ingredients and toss. Close the lid and cook beef sirloin for 5 hours on High. Divide between plates and serve.

Nutrition:

Calories 229

Fat 8.7g

Carbs 1.2g

Protein 34.5g

Caraway Ribs

Preparation time: 15 minutes

Cooking Time: 4.5 Hours

Servings: 4

Ingredients:

- 15 oz pork spare ribs

- 1 ½ teaspoons caraway seeds

- ½ teaspoon cumin, ground

- ½ teaspoon sweet paprika

- ½ teaspoon garam masala

- ½ teaspoon dried oregano

- ½ teaspoon dried basil

- 1 tablespoon olive oil

- 1/3 cup water

Directions:

1. In your crockpot, mix the ribs with caraway seeds and the other ingredients. Close the lid. Cook the spare ribs for 4.5 hours on High.

Nutrition:

Calories 311

Fat 15g

Carbs 7.3g

Protein 20.1g

Dinner Lamb Shanks

Preparation time: 15 minutes

Cooking Time: 8 Hours

Servings: 3

Ingredients:

- 1 tablespoon of olive oil

- 3/4 cup of bone broth

- ½ teaspoon of rosemary, dried, crushed

- 1 tablespoon of melted butter

- 3 whole garlic cloves, peeled

- Salt and black pepper, to taste

- 3/4 tablespoon of Sugar-free tomato paste

- 1 ¼ tablespoon of fresh lemon juice

Directions:

1. Start by putting all the fixings into your Crockpot. Cover its lid and cook for 8 hours on Low settings. Once done, remove its lid and mix well. Garnish as desired. Serve warm.

Nutrition:

Calories 188

Fat 12.5 g

Carbs 4.9 g

Protein 14.6 g

Mint Lamb Roast

Preparation time: 15 minutes

Cooking Time: 3.5 Hours

Servings: 4

Ingredients:

- 1-pound rack of lamb, chopped

- 1 tablespoon minced garlic

- ½ teaspoon salt

- ½ teaspoon black pepper

- 1 teaspoon mint, dried

- ½ cup sour cream

- 1 tablespoon balsamic vinegar

- 2 tablespoons olive oil

- ½ teaspoon fresh rosemary, chopped

Directions:

1. In the crockpot, mix the lamb with garlic, salt, pepper and the other ingredients. Close the lid and cook lamb for 3.5 hours on High.

Nutrition:

Calories 370

Fat 26.6g

Carbs 6.3g

Protein 29.5g

Lightning Source UK Ltd.
Milton Keynes UK
UKHW022003210121
377486UK00003B/251